TRUMPed UP LIMERICKS

Fred Knitney

ARCHWAY PUBLISHING

Archway Publishing books may be ordered through booksellers or by contacting:

Archway Publishing
1663 Liberty Drive
Bloomington, IN 47403
www.archwaypublishing.com
844-669-3957

ISBN: 978-1-6657-5222-0 (sc)
ISBN: 978-1-6657-5223-7 (e)

Library of Congress Control Number: 2023920552

Print information available on the last page.

Archway Publishing rev. date: 11/17/2023

Trumpty-Dumpty and the truth he defies
Has told more than 30,000 lies
T'will certainly not delight 'im
Butt jump up and bite ' im
From which we can hope that he dies

Trumple-shitskin is a scary two-legged male
An orange-skinned two-legged whale
With a whine and a cry
He continues to defy
And hopefully he'll soon end up in jail

Trumpty-Dumpty the Orange Menace mass
Trumpty-Dumpty slipped 'n fell on the grass
No help from the right
They've lost their sight
Their heads are so far up his ass

We now know about Trump and his taxes
He's cheated and deducted to the maxes
Now he is dunned
For his phony refund
The IRS should shove the bill up his assets

Trump is now slowing the mail
We hope that at this he will fail
By voters rejected
And not re-elected
Should be convicted and sent off to jail

Let's send Trump, Melania, Ivanka
On a one way trip to Sri Lanka
Also Don, Eric, n' Kuch
With stakes up their tush
Even if they don't really want'a

Trump is a man of only self-belief
Yet continues to cause so much grief
Bring him to his knees
Cuffed and arrested please
This liar, robber, con man and thief.

Get rid of Republicans and the Trumpster
Vote all of them out in one lump-fer
If they should return
More laws they will spurn
So let's just put all of them in the dumpster

Trump has a thing with his hair
Perhaps 'cuz his brain's not all there
Dyed blonde it hovers
Above what it covers
Just bullshit and lots of hot air

Trump wears long lengthy ties
Reaching almost to his thighs
He buttons his jacket
To cover his packet
But he can't conceal all his lies

Trump is a complete and total covidiot
If only he'd done just a little bit
Made less of a mess
Admit and confess
Then he should've resigned and up n' quit

The 2020 November federal election
Nears its new current presidential selection
For someone to lead
Provide what we need
And confirm D. J. Trump's total rejection

For Trump and his government "friends"
Who continue much action which offends
His family included
Lets not be deluded
They should all come to very bad ends

A bully a whiner, a liar and crook
Of all these Trump has the look
An ignorant asshole
Who's gathered a passel
Who all operate from the same book

Don Junior's a chip off the blockster
Thinks he's a political Rockstar
No brains in his head
They're lower instead
In the small head of his cock, sir

This is all about President Trump, sure
He's an ignorant, arrogant lump -ster
He may think he's hung
But its really his tongue
Which he should stuff up his own rump, sir

Trump is a true son-of-a-bitch
Who should really cash in his chits
Let's strip him down
Drive him from town
With feathers, some tar and some pitch

As for Moscow Mitch and his bitch
They should be dismissed with a twitch
Then if we're lucky
Returned to Kentucky
And dumped in a roadside ditch

Trump has insulted the military
But as usual lies to the contrary
All were poor choosers
Suckers and losers
He said so where they're dead and buried

This is for all those DJ Trump folks
Who've bought into his own lying hoax
He's down the tube
A boob and a rube
Let's hope he keels over and croaks

Introducing President Trump, Donald John
Who has mastered the art of the con
He screws many others
Including his brothers
From the conspiracist group QAnon

Trump claims mail-in ballots are prolific
His efforts to discredit them are olympic
But everyone notes
That's how he votes
So why believe the Orange Menace prick.

Trump says there will soon be a vaccine
Yet he knows nothing of science we've seen
Didn't he suggest
It would be best
To inject bleach or take hydroxychloroquine

Trump lies like that rug on his head
T'would be better by far if he'd instead
Put his head up his ass
Inhale the foul gas
Then be silenced and drop over dead

Trump is a confirmed liar, a bully and thief
He'll ne'er change or turn over a new leaf
So let's vote him out
This Mouth of the Lout
And hope his remaining days are brief

Time for Trump is now running short
Too bad his mom just didn't abort
He wouldn't be here
No need to fear
He'd be less than a sneeze or a snort

Should Trump die by covid or gunshot
No matter the manner how he's got
Just bag 'im
And tag 'im
Then dump him in the ground to rot

Since Trump won't cover his face
Let's send him to outer space
He won't pollute
'Cuz for this commute
We'll wrap him uptight just in case

I don't want Trump to wear a mask
I want him to ignore this simple task
Let him be dead
Not sick in bed
Should anyone ever bother to ask

Trump said soldiers are losers and suckers
If they live they're only good-luckers
Get rid of him
And all his kin
They're all rotten motherfuckers

The House finally did manage to impeach
As Trump tried to bribe Ukraine and reach
A smear of Biden
While he's in hidin'
Crimes of his own the son-ov'a-beetch

And all the Republican's silence
Will be met with voter defiance
Put new people there
Those who will care
With good will sense and reliance

Trump's family is now quite bereft
He's got covid and short of breath
But we can hope
This covidiot dope
Earns his own well- deserved death

Trump's touting a rigged phony election
Regardless of its state of perfection
Head to the courts
As results he aborts
'Cuz he can't face loss and rejection

As for the first presidential debate
Trump spewed only venom and hate
Biden defied him
And all his lyin'
Now the voters will determine their fate

The other nations should all get together
To decide how, now, when or whether
To shut out the US
Let'm drown in their mess
Then sanction, isolate n' relationships sever

Trump has finally succumbed to the virus
It's oh so delicious and oh so desirous
Sick in his bed
If he becomes dead
We can dispose of this human detritus

Prepare cells for Trump's family at Rykers
They're nothing but thieves, bums n' pikers
And after the trial
In jail a long while
To be entertained by Hell's Angels n' bikers

Trump's a historic mass-murdering figure
And the pandemic has been the real trigger
Thousands are dead
Should be him instead
So far only Stalin's totals are bigger

As for DJT and his family we're hopin'
We'll soon be no more time devotin'
To the cult craze
Of Trump's criminal ways
All deceit, cheating, theft, fraud in the open

Trump claims he is the Chosen One
And now he's making a second run
A November defeat
Means he can't repeat
So fuck off DJ Trump you're all done

Trumpty-Dumpty the Orange Menace mass
Trumpty-Dumpty slipped 'n fell on the grass
No help from the left
They've clogged up his cleft
With Republican heads so far up his ass

Trump is 421 million in debt
And there's certainly more you can bet
The US should claim
Take all in is name
Until the books show he's at zero net

Lets help Donald become a MacDonald
Work for minimum wage to help Ronald
Eat what you wish
Fries, burgers and fish
And also include Graham and McConnell

Trump went to a fund raiser and knew
He'd been exposed but to hell with you
Just give me the bucks
I know that it sucks
But I'll share covid virus with you, too

We can hope that Trump's seriously ill
That he gets it much worse even still
To horribly die
But never to lie
In state but an unmarked landfill

Trump owns hotels and many a resource
Constantly mentions them only to endorse
But he'd rather by far
Be cheating at par
Hitting his balls on his Florida golf course

Trump is rarely seen with his face masked
Watching TV instead of the job he's tasked
He won't address
The tracing mess
Especially if the "fake media" has asked

Trump needs to learn about good health
Observing science protects, not great wealth
With his persistence
Without mask or distance
A ripe victim for covid's silent stealth

Trump went to Walter Reed to recover
It took his own infection to discover
No personal boon
He's not immune
And guilty of the spread like no other

At the WH super-spreader by POTUS
To introduce a new judge for SCOTUS
They ignored the science
In their stupid defiance
Now many more are infected plus FLOTUS

Trump along with Lindsey and Mitch
Was whelped by an evil political witch
In governing join
Two sides of a coin
This trio of corrupt sons of a bitch

Trump's a stupid man of many false fronts
Hooked on women's boobs and their *****
Grab 'em by the pussy
Pinch 'em on the tushy
A sociologically sick predator and dunce

I think I'm about out of rhymes
For Trump and these covidian times
Hard to express
How bad the mess
He's created with his arrogance and crimes

Trump ignored science and now he's sick
This arrogant and stupid New York hick
An ignorant lout
Let's vote him out
And be rid of this pathological prick

Trump should be jailed, kept in seclusion
For spreading covid lies with profusion
Thinks given the nod
That he's really a god
So deep and dangerous is his delusion

News of Trump's condition remain
They're a continual confusing refrain
Doctors don't confide
What facts do they hide
Flush the Hippocratic oath down the drain

No matter the truth Trump's denying
That he speaks only falsehoods defying
As belief grows dim
No real trust in him
Though he said if I'm lying I'm dy.....

At the Presidential debate in Ohio
Trump was rude to Biden me-oh-my-oh
Always interrupting
Stupidly disrupting
Send this political pig back to his sty-oh

Donald still leads his hysterical base
Can't get enough of his lies and orange face
They hang on his words
Eat his political turds
To America's embarrassment and disgrace

After Trump's long forgotten and dead
Left the country that he should have led
His library for books
About he and his crooks
Will be the only time that he is well read

We've learned that Trump's not very well
He's caught the covid virus, do tell
He's behaved badly
Let's all cheer gladly
Perhaps he'll die and reside beneath hell

When Trump is retired please don't mention
Giving one penny to his old age pension
Placed in a cell
Underneath hell
Where he can rot for his crimes in detention

Trump was given an experimental drug
So I've got covid he said with a shrug
What's the big deal
I'm a big wheel
Better if they had just pulled his plug

Trump has covid but just gave a shrug
Swept his diagnosis under the rug
Said I'm not sick
Get me outta here quick
But I want more of that damn special drug

Trump's joyride to wave to his supporters
Was to appear before cameras and reporters
Just had to be seen
The publicity fiend
Screw the doctors I'm the who gives orders

Trump's arrogance extends to the limit
The covid virus hasn't even dimmed it
For his personal psychosis
I think the dose is
A sulfuric acid enema, please give him it

Trump's eager to leave Walter Reed
Says it's something his ego don't need
Doesn't like the terms
There're too many germs
I need to be seen, I've an ego to feed

Trump's health generates such speculation
Which I approach with great trepidation
It's not too late, sir
Would really be great, sir
If you'd die for the sake of the nation

In November if Trump's re-elected
I'll be completely and totally dejected
T'will end the US
Descend to the abyss
And the whole world will be infected

As the 3rd of November draws near
The entire world's watching it's clear
We can all hope
To be rid of this dope
Trump's international footprint's nu-cu-lear

Seems Trump's covid will not long endure
About his symptoms doctor's seem unsure
There's a new drug batch
So please let him catch
More diseases and then die from the cure

Trump recommends injecting some bleach
Taken internally it can be sure to reach
All our insides
And really besides
It's available to all and could fill the breech

I'm sick of this unpresidential buffoon
Please let's get rid of him soon
Nothing is hipper
Than a wood chipper
For such a mobster, a thief and a goon

Trump's covid response is systemic
Though he knows the virus's endemic
He said so what
I can sit on my butt
While America succumbs to the pandemic

Since his infection there's been little tracing
To find all the others that covid's embracing
He doesn't care
If here or there
As through the entire population it is racing

Trump's infected many and that's up to par
Like Lee, Johnson, MacEnany and Barr
President of Notre Dame
Kelly Ann Conway the same
And others known and unknown - so far

Enough with this fat jerk in Washington
Writing Trump limericks is still lots of fun
Where is the assassin
Shoot him in the ass'n
Then we'll all thank the NRA for the gun

And what about Vice-President Pence
He's been exposed but no need for suspense
Rarely heard or seen
He won't quarantine
A 2-fer duo for the pandemic's resurgence

Please reject Trump and Mike Pence
To re-elect them defies all good sense
YES to disapprove
And YES again to remove
This Republican ill-mated Duo of Dense

There's a debate between Pence and Kamala
An impala in the same cage with a koala
So go take a hike,
You're out-classed, Mike
Where Kamala leads you can't folla'

Trump's trying to slow down the mail
Though it already crawls like a snail
Ballots are delayed
Because he's afraid
His re-election bid's going to fail

To hell with the electoral college
Republicans will turn it on edge
Votes under duress
Create a big mess
And refuse the results to acknowledge

Trump tells so many fact-checkable lies
Wants you to believe it's truth in disguise
We must refute 'im
Silence and mute 'im
Or just gag him with one of his long ties

For his handling of the covid pandemic
Trump is really a one person mandemic
It wasn't desirous
But he caught the virus
His complete failure to act is damned epic

Trumps says all those ladies are liars
But for his lies there aren't many buyers
Screw his denial
Put him on trial
Conviction is definitely what he requires

On the day of November third
Please let your voices be heard
There is no defence
For team Trump and Pence
Vote and give America the last word

Mike Pence is a milk toast and chump
From Indiana to Washington's dump
Has no ideas
Just tries to please
With his nose so far up Trump's rump

I'm a stable genius Trump has stated
And this idea could surely be debated
This ignorant jerk
And his arrogant quirk
Sports a brain which is self-over-rated

Donald Trump of himself is the adoringist
With the truth he's a verbal contortionist
He's badly behaved
We might have been saved
If his mom and just seen an abortionist

What's with this blonde mop of hair
And what's underneath it up there
There are no brains
Nothing remains
Only a hole filled with noxious hot air

Trump's a joke on the international stage
The premier clown and buffoon of the age
A prolific liar
Just like his sire
And America's first true King of Outrage

For the KKK and all the white supremacists
Trump's rhetoric seems to support and assist
He says he ain't
But he bears the taint
Of a white right-wing nutcase and racist

Saying Kamala's a monster and communist
Trump should definitely cease and desist
The statement's a lie
And from a guy
Whose brain places him among the stupidist

Trump's lies are a bad character trait
When speaking all he does is fabricate
And if he should die
Everyone will know why
Washington won't allow him to lie in state

In office if Trump should happen to die
Few would cry or even ask why
Send his body home
Not placed under the dome
Find some other state where he can lie

Mike Pence lives in a parallel universe
His demeanor is condescending or worse
His verbal description
Is a false depiction
For he often describes reality in reverse

The Michigan militia has ranted and wailed
But their missions in Lansing have failed
There was no warfare
Soon to enjoy state welfare
When they're tried convicted and jailed

The militia tried to snatch Gretchen
But before they could get to the fetchin'
The plot was uncovered
They were discovered
And the FBI was able to catch 'em

If you ever have Trump as a client
He'll never listen or remain silent
Acts like a pig
An ego so big
Always ignorant, arrogant, and defiant

Trump wants to erase everything Obama
Every decision, every act, every comma
Argued with scorn
Where Barak was born
He's the villain in his own melodrama

Mr. Trump you've done a bad job, sir
You've failed and really played hob, sir
Of all the Presidents
And White House residents
You've been the first thug and mobster

Trump's like the gift that keeps giving
The US population's who he's been shiving
Put us at ease
Help the US please
So much better if he's no longer living

On that long awaited November day
Please send Trump packing and on his way
Warned in advance
Don't take a chance
Shoot the bastard if he tries to stay

Please vote and send Trump from DC
Just imagine how good it could be
Here's to Joe Biden
With Kamala beside 'im
To save the land of the brave and the free

Comparing Trump to all former Presidents
He's a one man pandemic and pestilence
If he dies we can revel
When he meets the Devil
He'll likely destroy hell with his residence

Vote out this idiot on November third
Wave him g'bye with a 3-finger bird
After we sack 'im
Let's send him packin'
These last four years have been absurd

The Mueller report hit the news with a thud
Made Trump appear an orange Elmer Fudd
Despite no conviction
The lengthy depiction
Of crimes should've been nipped in the bud

Trump says Obama spied on his campaign
But he's always treated Barak with disdain
Hates that he's black
Repeats the same tack
With his constant false birther refrain

For Mr. Trump's intelligence we can state
No evidence of important knowledge to date
Added up then
Barak's a ten
Go piss up a tree, Trump, ur-in-ate

If Trump doesn't win he's in trouble
His debts and his crimes just a couple
Reasons for disgrace
Reside in a barred place
It will all burst his bubble to rubble

When Trump's done the court's should file
All the charges they can for the trial
Include his kids
Pull out the skids
Incarcerate them all a long while

When Trump leaves DC for Trump Tower
Sits on his gold throne's seat of power
Knows the bill's coming due
Hey, they're coming for you
But he'll do nothing but whine and cower

Trump's a jerk but thinks that he's it
When he can't get his way throws a fit
Sitting on his gold throne
He moans and he groans
Finished crapping he's still full of shit

Trump was born without humor
That's a known fact not a rumor
What the heck
That thing on his neck
Is absent an intelligent roomer

Trump says he was cured by Regeneron
Fauci's not sure that it's truth or con
But Trump's alive
Continues to thrive
As America's prime leader and moron

From the moment Trump descended the stair
All bullshit, bad manners and flair
I couldn't but wonder
What was there under
That silly glued flop of blonde hair

Trump's knowledge of the world is tragic
He knows little of the world's geographic
Claims he's alive
For he doesn't drive
Because he always gets lost in the traffic

Trump's plans to win the election in court
Mail-in ballots SCOTUS judges must abort
No matter the amount
They just shouldn't count
If the judicial system's his final resort

Trump constantly declares its fake news
Claims it's political and personal abuse
He wants to suppress
And muzzle the press
Unless, of course, it agrees with his views

Trump doesn't drink so he's not drunk
But he romps and stomps in a blue funk
Hates the fake media news
They disparage his views
Because everything he says they debunk

Sometime in November we'll see
Who will govern the land of the free
Hope Biden does win
Not the man of orange skin
Please replace this human debris

When Mr. Trump's out of office and busted
By the IRS and all the ladies he lusted
He'll look in your eye
Tell one more big lie
After thousands how can he be trusted

Try Trump, convict and take all his money
A 300 pound cellmate won't be funny
He doesn't care
How you ended up there
Just bend over and he'll call you honey

Clad in red MAGA hats and blue T-s
200 not 2000 were there at his knees
Those not there
Were safer elsewhere
In case he sneezed and spread the disease

If Trump while he's speaking should sneeze
With no mask means he's created a breeze
There's little doubt
That what comes out
Could infect you with covid disease

Trump's doctor's reports don't make sense
Unclear answers make everyone tense
He won't be believed
We won't feel relieved
Til he spends 3 days in bed with Mike Pence

Trump's home is his Mar-a-Lago retreat
Where he'll live after November 3rd's defeat
If all his pleas fail
And he ends up in jail
He'll just suck on a new government teat

If Trump loses you'll hear his loud groans
More reasons than a loss for his moans
Unable to hide from
The lenders who will come
Demanding payment for millions in loans

I haven't heard anyone who's disputin'
That Trump's loves Vladimir Putin
To admire this knave
Send both to the grave
Where they can meet Grigori Rasputin

The Dems want SCOTUS hearings delayed
'Cuz of the Affordable Act n' Roe v. Wade
If Barret's confirmed
The Dems are burned
And the SCOTUS move to the right is made

On 28 January Trump was told so he knew
That the covid virus pandemic could kill you
But he lied instead
And publicly said
Don't worry it's no worse than the flu

I really can't stand Mister Trump's speeches
The lies and the false conclusions he reaches
Not just for a few
But for everyone true
He's always been too big for his breeches

Trump claims he mastered the art of the deal
But beware of believing this con man's spiel
Hold on to your locket
Best protect your pocket
He's most likely planning a big steal

Trump says he's a great man of business
But the man's so full of shit and duplicitus
So many times bankrupt
We know he's corrupt
He ignores our complaints and dismisses us

Mister Trump, I've had a great vision
When the judge gives his final decision
You will be gone
For all you done wrong
And spend the rest of your days in prison

Compared to the first 44 Presidents
We can state with no thought or hesitance
We must have been cursed
You have been the worst
Farewell, goodbye, enjoy your jail residence

Mr. Trump we don't wish you in hell
Another place will serve just as well
Your roommate's named Bubba
And he's gonna' lov'ya
Every night in your small prison cell

Mister Trump the polls say you're losin'
When you do it should not be confusin'
We think you'll do well
In an 8x10 cell
Which prison won't be of your choosin'

DJT should be arrested n' charged because
He's also ignored the emoluments clause
For all that he's received
By the US treasury retrieved
Then fine him and confine him for cause

DJT has broken far more than one law
And he says with a sneer and guffaw
There's been no charge
I'm still free and at large
And that really sticks in my craw

Trump's many disgressions rub me raw
We know he's broken more than one law
So put him in jail
With a really large male
Who says just shut up and open your jaw

Hey Mister Trump, up yours and screw you
Several guys in prison are waiting to do you
They're losers and hicks
But they've all got pricks
And when you arrive they'll stick it to you

On the 3rd we hope the voters defeat you
When the ballots are counted unseat you
Prison is all male
And all those in jail
In their own way will be happy to greet you

When Trump rents his name it's not free
At least thirty percent is his fee
Oh what a shame
They're removing his name
So place it free on the doors where we pee

I can't allow Trump's stupidity to pass
He's so full of bullshit and his own gas
He gets no more byes
Let's take all his lies
And shove them straight up his ass

Trump wants to pack the Supreme Court
He's expecting his vote will come up short
If the Dem count is best
The Republicans will request
The reverse of election totals and abort

After covid Trump's acting more ridiculous
His behavior and statements more ludicrous
His verbal outbursts
Have become even worse
About covid they're completely infelicitus

On the WH balcony posing like Mussolini
Trump looked stuffed n' filled with linguini
So heavy the makeup
The orange was caked up
But much better than him in a bikini

Remove Senate Republicans from the floor
Throw them physically out the door
They've spread their legs wide
Invited the Donald inside
Only function as the President's whore

If the Supreme Court reverses Roe v. Wade
There'll be a hell-uv-a price to be paid
Women may say
Sorry not today
And on you we'll just use a sharp blade

If Roe v. Wade is no longer in force
There'll be an increase in family divorce
If you don't wear a condom
You ain't going to get some
Or you'll have to search for a new source

Roe v. Wade affects women and maid
If reversed men face a price to be paid
Without a condom
They won't get none
And might wait a long time to get laid

Abortion laws affect all girls and women
But there are no laws which apply to men
Let's just suppose
The ladies propose
You'll need state permission to screw them

Roe v. Wade is a legal question quite hot
Best seriously consider you're support or not
Passed women say no
Tell you where to go
The screwing you'll get for what you got

When Trump is voted out of Washingtown
And this arrogant clown is brought down
No worries Don
In your life as a con
Orange blends with white, black and brown

Trump has been a disaster since his youth
Always lacked acquaintance with the truth
Can't change now
Wouldn't know how
Always a boor, a bully and uncouth

People cross the border in desperation
If caught the US places them incarceration
Women and children in cages
With no regard for their ages
And then they enforce family separation

Illegal immigrants entering as a last resort
Are caged n' separated from kids at the port
It's total insanity
A crime against humanity
And Trump should face charges in court

They look across the border at the US
The hopeful solution to their living mess
But how do they fare
Once they get there
Trump's decisions only add to their duress

Trump's orders at the border aren't vague
Incarcerate and place in a wire cage
For this humanity crime
He should do time
Or face trial at the World Court at the Hague

Donald likes to think he's a king
That all must kneel and kiss the royal ring
He was never appointed
But should be jointed
In a solitary prison cell in Sing Sing

Trump's whining and baby talk is noise
If jailed he would have no other choice
A sound proof cell
Would be better than hell
He'd be forced to listen to his own voice

Trump Republicans say not a word
State truth only when they can't be heard
Hardly adult
But part of the cult
And for them all I have is the BIRD

Trump loves MacDonald burgers and fries
When he orders they're always super-size
His gourmet taste
Ends up at his waist
His belly, his ass and his thighs

Instead of debate Trump had a Town Hall
Where he repeated the same lies and told all
I'm your best hope
Biden can't cope
With life, happiness and liberty for all

In the debate a fly landed on Mike's head
They love shit so it sat for a minute and fed
But we heard it say
As it flew away
I prefer the real stuff in the stable instead

The Republicans have all sold their souls
To Trump's cult and reading the polls
By the voter's decree
Some will depart DC
Go home and crawl into their holes

Please vote overwhelmingly en masse
And get rid of this snake in the grass
Remove this prick
Then take a big stick
And shove it straight up his ass

If the vote's a big Democratic landslide
Trump says he won't accept or abide
He'll go to court
To try and abort
The results and overturn them to his side

US women are preparing a new bill
If Roe v. Wade's overturned they will
Move for male chastity belts
Hold the keys 'til hell melts
Force all the men to take a derectil pill

The International Thug Club likes Trump
And if he were asked to join he would jump
But what did they say
No way Jose
You stupid, uninformed, ignorant, chump

The time for Trump's departure is close
Let the voters give him a strong dose
Give their approval
For instant removal
As he departs all should thumb their nose

Giuliani is one of Trump's legal tools
For lies, dirty tricks and breaking rules
The Russians have duped 'im
And Trump has used 'im
He's just a jester in Donald's court of fools

Trump ignores his US Intelligence info
Says he doesn't think or perhaps know
But he likes Mr. Putin
And won't be refutin'
If Vlad says it's true he'll never say no

Putin and Kim Jong Un have the last word
Trump's the dumbest leader they ever heard
They pretend they're fond
Of the orange-faced dumb blonde
While they laugh and give him the bird

In November the US has a chance to renew
With Trump gone there'll be a fresh view
He cannot stay
Must go away
From the WH on Pennsylvania Avenue

If Trump's defeated my words will be few
It's a chance for the United States to renew
As he goes away
We'll stand up and say
So long, dasvidanya, so long and fuck you

Mr. Trump's brought the country to ruin
When he's gone he will soon be viewin'
The world from Florida
But it'll just be more-a-da
Same lies, bullshit and verbal screwin'

Trump's outrageous lies have increased
Will probably continue 'til he's deceased
So cut off his tongue
And pierce his lung
Until all that hot air's been released

Take all Trump's money and reduce him
Being a pauper will hardly enthuse him
An ex-President in jail
His residence won't fail
To have inmates lined up to seduce him

When Trump's tried and sentenced to jail
The inmates will have a lotto ticket sale
You can cancel all bets
What the winner gets
Is a piece of DJT's Presidential tail

Defeated Trump will lose political power
Send him back to NY and Trump Tower
When he looks out the window
The BLM street sign below
Will make his blood curdle and turn sour

Biden's choice of Kamala Harris was slick
Gives the voters a black and white pick
On the other pair
You get the hair
Of a blonde prick and a white-haired hick

Mr. Trump you're about to go down
In defeat turn in your feigned crown
As many have supposed
To all you're exposed
As a loud-mouthed buffoon and a clown

Trump lies and conspiracies are outrageous
They're meant to confuse and engage us
It's a false view
Of what's really true
To ignore him is morally courageous

Mr. Trump you'll sure give the devil a scare
What a colorful addition for him down there
White skin, blonde hair a start
Then orange face and black heart
But all will burn with a lovely red flair

Mr. Trump's tone is obnoxious and intrusive
His verbal statements so false and inclusive
He tries to disguise
What's behind all his lies
With the truth he's so verbally abusive

Trump said we'd win so much we'd get sick
Then I guess he'd better do something quick
From where I sit
He's accomplished shit
Only empty promises that don't do the trick

Trump bragged about his massive tax break
About what a great difference it would make
Little help for the bottom
Poverty's nearly got 'em
And the one percent just increase their take

Trump's tax relief bill closed the doors
On the middle-class and others by scores
The rich got their remittance
While you received a pittance
Once again they lied and stuck it up yours

Trump has declared this as character week
And his words were well-written and sleek
But he doesn't believe 'em
Just wants you to receive 'em
There's no hint of honor in this freak

Trump's nickname should really be Bozo
He's colorful and shouts and blows so
This neanderthal yokel
Who's so rabidly vocal
Is an idiot and everyone knows so.

On 3 November let's Trump's fate seal
Including his family would be quite ideal
Dump 'em in a deep well
Or send them to hell
Donald will say, hey Satan, let's make a deal

If you take a trip down Memory Lane
When the days were much more urbane
Trump wasn't President
Or White House resident
The world and our politics more sane

Trump's words and behavior are so base
Lacking empathy without hint of taste
He is a profanity
A blight on humanity
An international embarrassment 'n disgrace

Trump is without borders and tasteless
Hard to find anyone more disgraceless
A foul mouthed lout
He must be turfed out
The first name on a clear thinkers hate-list

If Trump's re-elected what a tragic blunder
The USA will be destroyed, torn asunder
I'm really believing
It's time to be leaving
I've always wanted to go down under

If Trump's nonsense constantly assails ya'
He's insulting and continuously fails ya'
Consider with no delay
Pack all your bags today
And take a trip down under to Australia

When we need him, where is the assassin
This President is beyond normal harrassin'
He encourages violence
There's minimal defence
Please vote him out and do his ass in

Enroll Mr. Trump in a home for senior care
Let him remain to rot away and die there
With no policy he will
Allow covid to kill
Many more so it seems only fair

Trump considers himself a brilliant star
But he's measured by such a low bar
That most populations
Of all the world's nations
Are smarter and more intelligent by far

Trump wine, steaks, university are a sham
They're phony and like every other scam
But he feels no shame
When he loans his name
Takes the money and doesn't give a damn

If you're famous they'll let you do anything
Trump's taped words had a salacious ring
Women were furious
Had thoughts injurious
Many suggested removing his orange thing

Trump's mouth is like an open cesspool
He lies, calls foes bad names, thinks its cool
But he doesn't savor
If you return the favor
And has no clue he's an international fool

Rome burned while Nero played fiddle
Trumps's done similar and it's not a riddle
Just need to remember
When it's November
Throw his fat ass on a hot griddle

Trumps's done nothing about infrastructure
If asked says please don't interrupt, sir
You are very rude
And be sure to include
The fake media which is so corrupt, sir

For DJT there's no satisfactory explanation
The loss of face and disgrace to the nation
So pass the word
Vote November 3rd
And send him on a permanent vacation

Trump's kids are chips off the same block
All of their time is short on the clock
They were all whelped
It can't be helped
That they all came from such poor stock

Trump continues his outrageous attacks
On the news media, Biden, and that's
A stupid decision
His verbal derision
Isn't supported or backed up by facts

Trump's losing even more of his mind
His claims more outrageous, we find
Covid is turning
Biden he's burning
It's just more political bump and grind

Trump attacked Fauci n' called him an idiot
But new x-rays show there's only a little bit
Left of Donny's brains
And what remains
Is infected and he really is a covidiot

Mr. Trump just doesn't come up to muster
Bad manners, stupidity n' ignorant bluster
Silence the bastard
We get the last word
Shut up and Trump it up your butt, sir

At last from Trump some good news
Said he might leave the US should he lose
A ticket one way
We'll donate today
And if he insists on a return we'll refuse

Mr. Trump you're verbal bombast is abuse
You represent the apex of human refuse
Either confined in a cell
Or sent straight to hell
But never again allowed on the loose

Mr, Trump the country has grown tired
As President you're no longer desired
We'll register the vote
And you should take note
We have clearly stated, YOU'RE FIRED

The Republicans are Trump's political herd
They kiss his ass and hang on each word
No matter what
Attached to his butt
They're giving the entire country the bird

Remove Trump's ears he doesn't listen
For the US only he has a proper vision
Strap him to a missal
And with this we'll
Send him into space on a one-way mission

Anticipating the start of the second debate
Hope Biden is able to destroy and relate
His positions clear
And make Trump fear
His bombast and lies are too little too late

President Trump is a liar and a cretin
From the early signs from where I'm settin'
The bastard's going down
Farewell to the clown
A major humiliation and defeat I'm a bettin'

Covid is bad and so many are ill
Thousands are dead and it surges still
Many more will die
But it's missing the one guy
That so many have hoped it would kill

Mr. Trump you're a complete, total asshole
And for you I propose a new role
Placed under ground
No longer around
Serving as fertilizer to help the grass grow

Mr. Trump you're the ultimate creep
There's nothing about you'd we keep
By sickness or gun
We'll accept either one
If it results in your permanent sleep

Thought covid virus was a great chance, sir
For all our prayers at last a good answer
But you survive
Remain still alive
Spreading more of your political cancer

We hope for a complete political disaster
On 3 November a Republican massacre
If millions turn out
You'll have the clout
So vote and make sure you make it occur

Mr. Trump I'm really mad and quite pissed
You got covid but escaped the death list
Sorry you survive
Remain still alive
When thousands of good people are missed

When something is squeaky we oil it
If the water goes bad we must boil it
All easy to fix
But I'd get my kicks
If I could flush Mr. Trump down the toilet

We need a good dose of Putin's poison
Then add some of Xi's special hoisin
Let the Republicans drink
Include Trump and I think
We could do him and all of his boys-in

Trump delights in his personal vanity
Can't see that his life's a real profanity
There is no place
In the human race
For one so devoid of humanity

Trump died and was sent down below
When he arrived the Devil said hello
You've been expected
But you are rejected
I have higher standards, you know

Trump claims he's a great business man
But prison forbids what you wish you can
You have no say
You do it their way
They're going to give you the business, man

Trump died and his soul left this earth
When the Devil assessed his real worth
Said not looking good
It probably would
Have been better if you'd died at birth

His time on earth was such a poor showing
That Mr. Trump had no way of knowing
The hells gate sentry
Said, sorry, no entry
It's much further below that you're going

Donald Trump still has a large following
In all his lies n' bullshit they're wallowing
Results in poor diet
And I don't buy it
The cesspool of crap that they're swallowing

Only a few more days remain 'til the day
And if Trump loses but insists he will stay
Call out the troops
And if he regroups
Drag him screaming and kicking away

In November should Trump happen to win
Things will be even worse than they've been
Too late for me
I'm eighty-three
So please look after my next of kin

60 Minutes and Trump did not agree
It was disgusting yet amusing to see
The bully came out
It was a total rout
Pull his plug, and not the one on his TV

On 3 November what a joy it will be
If Trump's defeated and we all see
From the WH he's evicted
But if tried and convicted
The parasite's still living off you and me

Say goodbye to Donald and Melania
Your departure days are soon upon ya
We must have been cursed
'Cuz you've been the worst
Pack your bags, get out, dasvidanya

The famous portrait of Dorian Gray
Has certainly met its match today
No pic of this louse
In the White House
Burn it and let the ashes blow away

Trump claims he's a business tycoon
But he owes millions and they're due soon
When they take what he's got
He won't be feeling so hot
They'll take his ass-ets from this buffoon

In private Trump grins and shakes his head
These stupid fools hang on everything I said
It's quite incredible
Although it's inedible
They'll swallow all the bullshit they're fed

Trump's guilty of negligent homicide
More than one million US citizens have died
When history is written
He'll be sittin'
Near the top of the list of most vilified

They gather unasked to shout and to cheer
No social distancing and Trumpster so near
Another super-spreader
And more will be deader
B'cuz they stupidly attended a rally here

Get rid of this orange-faced lying blonde
No art of the deal but the art of the conned
He's taken you in
Got under your skin
This wolf in sheep's clothing he's donned

Trump promises to look after your needs
But it's really upon you that he feeds
Why can you not see
His only interest is "ME"
And he'll take and take 'til the US bleeds

About Trump my thoughts are so malicious
T'would be fantastic and quite propitious
Make an art of the meal
For a great jungle deal
Perhaps cannibals might find him delicious

I want to see Trump brought down so low
Let every citizen who wants strike a blow
After the last one
When all is done
Take all his possessions including his dough

Trump university, steaks, wine 'n bedsheets
Are only a few of his business defeats
Make this election
Another rejection
To make sure that he ne'er again repeats

November 3rd is here at last
Seemed slow but now so fast
To Trump farewell
FY go to hell
The reign of dis-ass-ter is finally past

Election night is here and no landslide
Early predictions and polls are defied
It must be noted
That so many voted
A winner will take longer to decide

I'm stunned and unable to understand
Trump retains such support in the land
I think it's tragic
What is the magic
That convinces people he is so grand

The battle for the soul of the US of A
May or may not be settled Wednesday
Early ballots for Biden
May result in decidin'
That the people have sent Trump away

Counting continues and will soon choose
But if not in Trump's favor he will refuse
Challenge the amount
If for him not the count
He'll ask the courts to not let him lose

Hour after hour it continues to go
Voting totals are bouncing to and fro
People going manic
Campaigns in panic
'Cuz the final vote takes so long to know

Consider only the current map and the math
Proves Trump has less votes than Biden hath
Oh please make it true
For the red, white and blue
Then we can take deep a breath and laugh

Tension is increasing by minute and hour
Donald appears to be hot under the collar
Gets under his skin
Count says no win
So we can send him back to Trump Tower

The vote counts keep coming in
But no decision concerning a win
Vote counting for more days
Patience for this lengthy phase
The margin of success could be thin

Trump always appears quite dapper
But we'll wipe you off of the map, sir
You're not the chooser
When declared the loser
We'll flush you n' yours down the crapper

Here marks the end of Trump's oligarchy
Biden says "Enough with all this malarkey"
Out with the goon
The joke, the buffoon
We're establishing an entirely new hierarchy

Here cometh a Trump temper tantrum
Easy to understand where it comes from
He's going down
Will have to leave town
Give him his gesture with YOUR thumb

I've got Nevada and Georgia on my mind
Where there are more votes to be mined
Count them all
Let the chips fall
Until the totals leave no more to find

Goodbye Mr. Trump but not farewell
To fare well is not what I wish but hell
To put you on welfare
Let all your kids share
Then a small jail cell would be just swell

Trump's Presidential portrait was finished
Planned to join others far more distinguished
But for the wall
Make it real small
To the size of a postage stamp diminished

Hello to Donald and his mega-dollar suit
Enough votes are in to loudly refute
Sing your sad song
Time you were gone
The US citizens have just given you the boot

My brother expects Trump to be President
Thinks SCOTUS will overturn voter intent
How can they change
Or votes re-arrange
So Trump remains the White House resident

And on and on it continues to go
Lots of talking but counting so slow
Let the talking end
Accept the voting trend
And inform Donald of what he must know

At last what we already knew is proclaimed
And President Biden is now acclaimed
It took so long
Didn't want to be wrong
Because so many more votes remained

Trumplestiltskin is now Trumple- has-been
It's what happens when you don't win
The country is freed
But will Donald concede
No idea whether he will, if or when

Donald is suing and attempting to thwart
All the totals and votes which states report
Says fraud was large
No facts for the charge
It's all in his head and not for the court

I'm so happy Biden and Harris have won
But I want something more to be done
To rub Donald's nose
In the success of his foes
Until he reaches the drawer for a gun

We must soon fumigate the White House
To eliminate the stink of the current louse
Include his progeny
Set the house free
No trace of his kids or Donald and spouse

Donald is now beat and must at last answer
So many crimes n' misdeeds at a glance, sir
You operated corruptly
Will be convicted abruptly
Sent for a lengthy sentence in the can, sir

The Republicans are silent and waiting
While Trump is playing golf and deflating
The voting is done
Biden has won
And the Democrats are now celebrating

Mr. Trump you are removed and that's fine
Five years of you is far too much time
So glad you're pissed
But you won't be missed
Have crackers and paté with your whine

Nero played the fiddle while Rome burned
Trump golfed while the country yearned
For a competent leader
Not this bottom feeder
Whose ignorance is every day confirmed

So Donald you're no longer Mr. Big
For your hurt feelings we care not a fig
You've behaved like a child
Since the votes have been filed
Not a political elephant, you're really a pig

So we're happy to tell Trump goodbye
He's pissed and trying to understand why
Biden beat him
T'was not a whim
Now he's just that orange covidiot guy

Without proof Trump claims the election
Was stolen by Democrats and his rejection
Is not for real
And he will appeal
Hoping for the Supreme Court's interjection

We apologize to Peanuts and Charlie Brown
There's a new great orange pumpkin in town
But curry your fury
No need to worry
Voters have put this orange clown down

We are at last rid of this petulant man-child
His name calling and insults were so wild
No ifs, ands or maybe
Trump's an overgrown baby
And his Presidency has the office defiled

Mr. Trump refuses to give in and concede
For certain, more of him we don't need
The narcissist must accept
He's now a reject
And disappear so the country can proceed

While Trump whacks his balls on his course
Giuliani, Pompeo, McConnell are his source
The false sense of hope
For this egotistical dope
But voters have declared it's a divorce

Mr. Trump please pack your bags go away
To you we have nothing more to say
The verdict is in
You didn't win
There's no way you'll be allowed to stay

Poor Donny behaves like a spoiled brat
He sulks and plays golf in his red hat
While others must fight
And bring into the light
That there was no fraud and that's that

Then there's the DOJ and ol' Billy Barr
Prime ass kisser of Mr. Trump and so far
He's backed Donald's play
In more than one way
As if he were personal lawyer to the czar

Bill Barr really doesn't seem to understand
He works for the US not the Trump brand
Hey, are you kidding
I do Mr. Trump's bidding
And respond to each request and demand

Poor Donald appears so down and dejected
P'rhaps because he's been soundly rejected
Let Donny pout
He's definitely out
Thank the voters he was not re-elected

Trump's firing his staff right and left
And the chosen ones seem little bereft
They couldn't pass
Didn't kiss his ass
But in a small way shoved it up his cleft

The situation in Washington is contentious
Donny's on a tear because he resents us
Since he's been demoted
By those who voted
The poor sulking infant wants vengeance

Trump is facing considerable investigation
No excuse for his crimes against the nation
Convict the bastard
Too long he's mastered
His criminal activities with no litigation

Ivanka, Don Jr, Eric and the Trumpster
All were entitled since being a youngster
They take, never give
So let them all live
Where the landfill and all the dumps'er

Trump lost the election and's in denial
Hope his self-pity is politically suicidal
Send him to Egypt
Have his head dipped
Under de Nile's waters for a long while

Votes are in, Trump's reign has been flipped
He cries and he claims that he was gypped
Pack up your ties
Along with your lies
De-Nile is located in Egypt

The courts are waiting your arrival
As a poor President you've had no rival
From the White House evicted
In court tried and convicted
Hopefully there's no hope for your survival

Time to remove him from the White House
Let Trump whine, whimper and grouse
It's time to be rid
Of this poor man-kid
So lets evict both DJT and his spouse

So many court challenges have failed
The sources of good have prevailed
For Trump it's defeat
No chance to repeat
Time to be tried, convicted and jailed

For Trump there remains little hope
As he hides in the White House to mope
Can't understand how
He must leave it now
With defeat he's quite unable to cope

Trump's loss on 3 November was great
Many millions of votes filed on that date
The Electoral College
With full knowledge
Will most emphatically seal his fate

Trump said we would be tired of winning
He lost and his internal critics he's thinning
He must be tired
Because he's been fired
And this loss is hopefully just the beginning

Trump had his name tattooed on his ass
D on the left and N the right of the mass
Where is the "O"
Oh don't you know
In the middle right where he passes gas

Poor Mr. Trump lost and refuses to yield
By seven million votes his fate was sealed
Now to the trials
To expose his wiles
Convicted and sentenced by what is revealed

For Trump the bad number is clearly 45
And you ask at this how did we arrive
It may sound abhorrent
But some swear a warrant
Should be issued for him dead not alive

The Donald is a child and a whimp
70,000 dollars for hair so he can primp
Such a prima donna
Yet the right wanna'
Continue to serve as his political pimp

There's no doubt that Trump's made history
His election loss he still resists for he
Can't walk away
To face the day
That this overwhelming loss is no mystery

Withdrawing troops in Iraq and Afghanistan
Trump wants to bomb nuclear sites in Iran
But what he proposes
The military opposes
Please shut him up as fast as you can

Lindsay Graham is a symbol of white trash
Such a flipflopper it makes your teeth gnash
He kisses Trump's bum
Until his lips hum
His request to Georgia was illegal and rash

Trump and the Republicans must end
Their election nonsense and bend
Voters have spoken
The system's not broken
But Donald and his allies still offend

Republicans are undermining the election
Saying the results are an illegal confection
Giuliani's going to court
Democratic voting to thwart
So far only embarrassment and rejection

Giuliani sweat and his hair dye dribbled
Down his cheeks as the reporters scribbled
Thank God the guy
Didn't unzip his fly
Hasn't pulled it out and publically piddled

Chavez was dead 7 years, but a conspirator
So said Sydney Powel so we need to explore
How this legal dunce
Donald Trump fronts
His challenge to the election and more

Rudi, Oh Rudi what has happened to you
Once famed as mayor but current review
Says you are down
Another Trump clown
Only fit for your own cage at the zoo

Mr. Trump is now one for 32 in court
Rudi's legal claims are coming up short
And the judge can see now
That brown line on his brow
Means he's definitely down a full quart

Trump's legal challenges are only a spoof
The charges make Rudi a political goof
There is no relevance
When there's no evidence
And you come to court without proof

Please spare us all and commit suicide
Better for the US if you disappeared or died
Respect the democracy
Stop this hypocrisy
When you're gone we'll all be dry-eyed

A hole in his bottom and one in his head
One for shit and one where he's fed
For you it's clear
But for Donald I fear
These two are interchangeable instead

The Republicans continue their silence
Which can only be seen as defiance
It's become formal
To support the abormal
Of Trump's whims by their compliance

Trump ignores, disregards covid in defiance
He and his sycophants place total reliance
On medical quacks
And political hacks
Continue to reject truth based on science

Poor Rudi you have now fallen so far
You're a joke and no longer a star
Now your hair dye leaks
Dribbles down your cheeks
And you will soon be disbarred from the bar

The US experiences such political division
It's now facing some world-wide derision
The bastion of democracy
Now the home of hypocrisy
Can agree on no reasonable decision

Trump challenges the vote in Pennsylvania
He claims too much voter kleptomania
Votes were stolen
Counts were swollen
But Donald this is the US not Transylvania

Trump challenged the results in Michigan
Lost in court twice but one more pitch again
It too has been lost
His bogus case tossed
So all Donald can do is just bitch again

As for Trump's embarrassing legal team
Rudi and Sydney are hardly the cream
Claim after claim
No proof n' no shame
They're certainly not worth their per diem

Day by day it becomes more ludicrous
There's far too much fury and fuss
If aides tell him to stop it
To accept defeat and drop it
They are fired and thrown under the bus

President Donald Trump's fragile ego
Can't accept loss to his foe, Sleepy Joe
He mopes and he pouts
But has no more outs
So it's time to concede, pack his bags n' go

Poor Donald is down in the dumps
He lost and can't take his lumps
Four years so wrong
At last he'll be gone
And take with him all of the Trumps

Republican silence has been ever so loud
Hunkered and wrapped in Trump's shroud
They all come up short
Because they support
And history will not write them up proud

I wish I could dig a hole deep enough
Fill it with politicians and their guff
Specifically Republicans
Without their pros 'n cons
Buried deep with all their political stuff

Mitch lost most of his marbles yet he talks
But we still ear them rattle when he walks
Such power in a dunce
And maybe just once
Kick him where it hurts until he squawks

As for Lindsay Graham, that political whore
Yes sir, what would you like me to be for
He'll go either way
Tell him what to say
He's proven himself rotten to the core

Lindsay Graham is a southern trash cracker
A switch-hitting Donald Trump backer
He lies in his teeth
There is little beneath
This Republican political hack and slacker

There's a banana republic south of Canada
All the Republicans need to take a miranda
For their linguistic abuse
With the truth they're so loose
Nothing but bald-faced lies and propaganda

Trump has now pardoned Michael Flynn
The NSA in Trump's late admin
Guilty 'cuz twice lied
I was tricked he cried
Turkey's half million just increased his sin

As for the 2020 massive election fraud
We must be overwhelmingly awed
No proof uncovered
Nothing false discovered
With millions involved we must applaud

Dem's stole the election that was Trump's
Rigged machines n' and major vote dumps
The FBI and Justice
Were surely part of this
I won but lost, so I'll fire all these chumps

Trump bilked 2 million bucks from his base
To recount the ballots in Georgia just in case
The mistakes favored Biden
His lead would only widen
By 89 votes and Donald lost more face

Hey Donald we really feel sad for you
But we offer a good deal for you two
Please depart with your spouse
For a new public "house"
Where your 3 older kids can reside, too

Trump's wallowing in self-pity
Now ain't that too bad 'n tough titty
The car's full of gas
So grab your sorry ass
And leave America's capitol city

Trump's thinking of running in 2024
No idea why as he's just out the door
He'll be a convicted felon
And not doing so well n'
We'd really prefer to see him no more

The Attorney General of Texas is now suing
To remove votes of five states and renewing
Claims of cheating
Because Biden was beating
Just more Republican-Trump snafuing*

Trump's ass is the biggest seen on a puppet
'Cuz so many Republican heads are up it
They followed the suit
To give five states the boot
Cancel their votes, tell democracy to fuck it

Trump's arrogance and head is so swollen
He was cheated and the election was stolen
It's a Biden defeat
I cannot be beat
And that's perfume not shit in my colon

Trump's pandemic plan requires reliance
On quacks and charlatans in their defiance
Without expertise
Present their decrees
But no reference to fact or true science

For all the Trump henchmen and enablers
All the Republican cheats, liars and fablers
Loud in their silence
In support of tyrants
Should get the shaft from their neighbors

America has reached a new point of arrival
And this state is a serious time of deprival
Abandon current trends
Non-partisan politics ends
To protect the US and democracy's survival

Hey Donald, it's time to face up to your past
All the crimes and the lies you've amassed
You'll be convicted
Your freedom restricted
When you face Lady Justice at last

Donald will soon be a convicted felon
How many crimes and lies there's no tellin'
And then a small cell
His personal hell
He'll be dragged there screamin' and yellin'

Donald Trump's about to be defanged
He should be racked, tortured and hanged
This orange headed dork
Will face the State of New York
Be criminally and judiciously gang-banged

Trump's leaving office in total disgrace
Still supported by Republicans and his base
But will they retreat
When in court he's beat
All the lawsuits and crimes he must face

Trump talks about a 2024 run again
If so please give the US a mulligan
4 years was enough
Painful and rough
You're all over, finished and done again

***S**ituation **N**ormal **A**ll **F**ucked Up

As the final days approach Donald's nervous
Shaky, irritable and tense on the surface
From the White House evicted
In the State of New York convicted
And we shouldn't pay for the Secret Service

And the nonsense continues in Washington
Republicans refuse to accept Biden's won
The January electoral battle
Will most certainly rattle
The base of democracy before they're done

Trump and his allies are attempting a coup
Treason, sedition by Trump's cult is true
The House and the Senate
Subvert law's basic tenet
Destroying democracy, the US, me and you

The rich and the powerful want more
If successful with Trump close the door
For all those below
Will deal a death blow
To equal justice and democracy's core

In Georgia and elsewhere such commotion
Conspiracy theory and lies much promotion
It's hard to explain
The falsehoods remain
And so many support them with devotion

The US appears to be nearing its end
Too much is broken rather than bend
No real surprise
Too little compromise
So much offensive bullshit to defend

6 January what will happen on this Tuesday
Will it become a Democratic news day
If Republicans win
Biden's troubles begin
As Mitch McConnell's power's still in play

While the election conspiracies abound
No evidence has been offered or found
Yet they louder profess
Demanding redress
Trying to drown out truth with their sound

What is the magic of this pathological idiot
He's convinced so many to support his shit
Among those he trounced
Their support is pronounced
What sane person could have predicted it

Trump's home as one of ex-President's
Mar-a-Lago is a social club not a residence
He signed in '93
And the locals agree
He shouldn't become one of the residents

It's really one for the presidential books
And it's just as bad as it criminally looks
Trump's pardons are many
And there aren't really any
Who aren't obvious and blatantly crooks

What crimes from self-pardon are smothered
One or everything now or future discovered
For any offense
It makes no legal sense
That any of Trump's crimes are not covered

If Trump can self-pardon for what he's done
He may have lost the election but still won
- Unless -
From the White House evicted
For insurrection convicted
Then he cannot make a 2024 run

Republicans gather like rats with blood thirst
Their rhetorical nonsense so well-rehearsed
Trump's stolen their souls
Left nothing but holes
So full of lies and bullshit they'll burst

Trump has stated he will not concede
The election was stolen and all that I need
Is your loud support
So we can abort
Mr. Biden's rejected and my win decreed

The election had to be rigged if I lose
No way the people would fail to choose
My personal perfection
For a Biden/Harris election
No no no they'll not DJ Trump refuse

Trump demanded three recounts in Georgia
If not there'll be much animosity towards ya
Find votes for me
Or you'll likely see
My supporters come down to waterboard ya

There'll be no peaceful transfer of powers
As Trump pouts, shouts and glowers
But the country is free
And happy to see
That Trump has been sent to the showers

The Electoral College votes are complete
All challenges have done nothing to deplete
A Biden/Harris win
The Democrats are in
And the Republicans and Trump in defeat

The Republicans and Trump are crying foul
Outrageous shouts and claims they howl
More lies and insults
Must reverse the results
Biden and Harris must throw in the towel

Threats and trouble are brewing on the right
Votes in the swing states are all in their sight
Clear all their aims
And the false claims
Now to the Senate to refute truth and fight

On the election Republicans have taken aim
Professing lies and deceit to their shame
But courts listened and said
Sixty-one times that instead
There is no evidence to support your claim

All members of Congress met to endorse
The Electoral College votes but of course
Senators Hawley and Cruz
Supported Trump's views
Championed Trump's fraud without remorse

The Electoral College count was disrupted
When an unruly right-wing mob interrupted
The doors were crashed
Windows were smashed
By Trump's speech exhorted and corrupted

Trump has now been twice impeached
The decision was quite quickly reached
He encouraged the riot
He cannot deny it
Convicted when the Capitol was breached

The mob was screaming "Hang Pence"
Making the insurrection more intense
Yet silent and white
He's been out of sight
Four years occupied in the past tense

Trump's been banned from Twitter
For posting lies and verbal litter
Silenced are his 145s
Can't invade our lives
As he sits in Florida so angry and bitter

Trump still has his hands on the throats
Of all the servile Republican goats
He dictates his demand
Tells them where to stand
While he sits on his fat ass and gloats

Trump will be tried again in the Senate
Lindsay Graham says he's ag'in it
It's not constitutional
Just a Dem retributional
But they say screw you LG let's begin it

The Feds are looking for MAGA rioters
Mostly ardent Trump allies and fighters
They ate it all up
Sipped from the cup
Consumed his bullshit as Trump dieters

MAGA rioters shat on the Capitol's floors
Broke through windows and smashed doors
Marched through the halls
Pissed on the walls
Looking for members to harm, of course

On January 6th the Capitol was attacked
And the Congressional chamber was sacked
Some remain at large
Others under charge
And saying they're not guilty, in fact

A Trumpian incited call for insurrection
Happened with his compliance and direction
He exhorted the groups
Harangued brain-washed troops
Stop the confirmation of Biden's election

Hawley, Cruz and Republican supporters
Did all they could as Biden election aborters
Arguments filled with flaws
No evidence for their cause
As confirmed by so many reporters

Trump's defeated, we should be rid of him
But such hopes have already become dim
Republicans kiss his ring
He still reigns as a king
And the political future of his party is grim

Marjorie Taylor Green was Georgia elected
By QUanon conspiracies and others injected
Spouts threats and lies
Under the guise
Of truth but she's politically infected

Representative Marjorie Taylor Green
Is one of the worst we've heard or seen
Georgia's bad choice
Gave her a big voice
But most of what she says is obscene

Representative Green has no committee
Now ain't that too bad and a pity
Should shut her mouth
Return to the South
No more sucking on the government's titty

Lou Dobbs has been fired from Fox News
For his conspiracies, lies and false views
The billion dollar lawsuit
They'll have to refute
For their consistent defiance of truths

Green said that Democrats should be shot
And there are more serous ideas she's got
A bullet for Pelosi's head
Better her own instead
She should be arrested right on the spot

Expel Senators Josh Hawley and Ted Cruz
Let others with integrity fill their shoes
They'll not reform
Remove their platform
Send them packing and silence their views

74 million Trump supporters are frightening
They need to be struck by truth's lightening
Destroy their derision
Give them truth's vision
Fill their brains with political enlightening

Trump always likes to brag about his wins
Impeached twice he's one of the has-beens
It should quench his thirst
He's achieved another first
Two times held responsible for his sins

But Congress has yet to find its way
Graham and McConnell still hold sway
And too many others
Of their Republican brothers
Are holding the Senate conviction at bay

The 2nd trial begins in due course
But Trump has shown no remorse
The Republicans say
They'll vote nay
And he'll be acquitted, of course

The impeachment decision is quite clear
It matters little what 100 jurors hear
The Democratic noes
Each Republican knows
Their yeses will acquit Trump again, I fear

Lies and conspiracies are all in plain sight
They've been heard on TV every night
And film for the eyes
So there is no disguise
No escaping this political blight

Trump's 2nd impeachment trial has begun
Despite all the verbiage when they're done
The country will lose
The Republicans will choose
And Trump once again will have won

US norms are moving in the wrong direction
Witness the present Trumpian insurrection
The Capitol was attacked
By Trumpsters was sacked
Lock them all up in a house of correction

Let's look forward to Trump's incarceration
May it be soon and of lengthy duration
Hold him to account
For the large amount
Of damage he's imposed on the nation

Three words from the lips of Bruce Castor
Made clear he's not a courtroom master
He was there to refute
And not prosecute
Another massive huge Trumpian disaster

Bruce Castor's a personal injury lawyer
Was his preparation sufficient to floor ya
The hire makes no sense
For Donald Trump's defense
He shouldn't have appeared before ya

Raskin and colleagues were right on point
Trump's duo unable the king to annoint
No cogent ideas
Just empty pleas
For his money he got a kick in his joint

That only six Republicans crossed the aisle
Is something perverse and quite vile
So frightened of Trump
Their heads up his rump
That their sacred oaths they so easily defile

Where was Rudy Giuliani in this mess
With no public statements we can but guess
That Trump's had enough
Of his nonsensical stuff
Forced to settle for even much less

What legal minds want to be painted
With helping Trump's attempt to be sainted
Let the Orange clown
Go up or go down
But they'll not participate and be tainted

As for the Senate Republican rank and file
Their positions determined for quite a while
History will note
Each Senator's vote
In Trump's second impeachment trial

The insurrection of the Capitol was chilling
But Trump's rants they were only fulfilling
So an out-of-control mob
Invaded, did their job
The result was destruction, fear and killing

Trump's 2nd impeachment trial is to begin
Bound to annoy and get under his skin
Said I don't care
I won't be there
Republican sycophants will see that I win

Trump continued to look all in the eye
What the hell is wrong with this guy
In himself so wrapped
He wants all entrapped
As he promotes and spreads the "Big Lie"

The Capitol mob broke in, shit on the floors
Pissed on the walls and smashed in the doors
The protectors inside
Resisted and some died
At the hands of this insurrectional force

US Senators and staffers were trying to hide
Protect their lives from the insurgents inside
Several cops injured
From beatings endured
One cop died and two more by suicide

Trump encouraged and incited the violence
He did so with full knowledge and reliance
I know how you feel
We must "Stop the Steal"
I depend on your rage and defiance

With violence and disgrace in full view
The nation and world experienced anew
The end of the hypocrisy
That Trump supported democracy
The people, the US, me and you

Trump didn't march to the Capitol at all
He returned to the WH and watched it fall
I like what I see
On my big screen TV
Why should I stop them with my phone call

For hours Trump enjoyed the confrontation
In the Capitol building and the sensation
Of the events he took note
And did nothing but gloat
During the mobs attack and desecration

Asked to speak Trump weakly condemned
And pretended he could not comprehend
The mobs excitement
At his incitement
His false condemnation did more to offend

The Democratic presentation was flawless
Trump and Republicans can take no solace
A lack of all interest
In what was witnessed
All the threats and the acts were so lawless

The political scene in the US
Is a disaster we must confess
Republicans stink
Aren't worth the ink
For supporting Trump's political mess

The Republicans have had their day
But Trump's grip on the party holds sway
The Orange colored Pig
Is still Mr. Big
While he continues to lie and betray

Trump is neither smart nor intelligent
A self-centered bully and belligerent
For all of his lies
He gets no more byes
His mouth washed out with deter-gerent

Lindsay Graham was born with two assholes
One in his butt, the other beneath his nose
They spew the same shit
As the chameleon twit
Can't seem to make either one close

Mitch stuck his head up his own ass
Acquitted Trump with others en mass
Then reversed the words
His mouth full of turds
And said Trump was guilty but crass

Trump thinks he's the head of a dynasty
That his geneology has the finest tree
It comes with a name
Of ambiguous fame
Butt…he's still just an ass minus – T

Hey Eric, you son-of-a-gun
Hear you might make a political run
We'll all have a laugh
With every gaff
But it really won't be any fun

Hey Lindsay and Don, a new case has risen
In Georgia and if there's a good decision
It's only seems fair
You two should share
The same cell when you're sent to prison

Trump is now pissed off with McConnell
If he lived closer Mitch he would pommel
Mitch protects the money
Like a bee after honey
So kiss my ass and get lost President Donald

D.C. is investigating the Capitol riot
So Trump and his friends should be quiet
What they all did
Was hardly hid
When subpoenaed they cannot deny it

Ted Cruz has received pointed reviews
Trump's sychophant made the BAD news
His response was quite bold
For those suffering in cold
He said "Leave,and go on a cruise"

Nikki Haley has fallen from Trump's grace
She blamed him for 6 January to his face
His attacks will be hard
But she'll disregard
And run her own GOP presidential race

And then there's Senator McCarthy
Trump turns him on with his car key
He kisses the ring
Bends knee to the king
And spouts all his bullshit and malarky

Trump's now permanently absent on Twitter
The result is less bullshit and less litter
His spelling was bad
His syntax was rad
But if you don't kiss his ass he gets bitter

Trump is really dumb and illiterate
Neither kind nor in the least considerate
If his kids turn their back
On this political hack
He will then be by his own litter bit

Trump's thinking of making a run again
Fox News can lie another ton for him
The Dems must prepare
Make sure to take care
If he runs he must be done in again

Trump is a sociological parasite
He cheats and steals with delight
And when he dies
His soul won't rise
Then he'll truly be out of sight

DJ Trump is a pathological liar and selfish
If he's convicted and jailed we can all relish
That locked in a cell
He'll not likely do well
For him we hope it will be hellish

As for Donald and all of the Trumps
They've played us all for such chumps
Gather all their words
Their political turds
And shove them straight up their rumps

What is Donald J. up to right now
And what about his silent frau
The lawsuits are comin'
No escape from 'em
And if convicted straight to the hoosegow

Trump continues to golf and pontificates
I'm still President he insists and so states
The end result
Is quite difficult
Separating the words from what he defecates

Trump still governs o'er his lunatic fringe
The fables and conspiracies make one cringe
No matter the lies
Told by these guys
They experience no guilt, not a twinge

If he's refused Donald plans to avenge
His warped psyche will pursue to all ends
Whether done or said
He'll be after your head
And never quit 'til he's had his revenge

The worst former President named Don
An embarrassing buffoon and moron
This ruthless bastard
Has truly mastered
The art of the big steal and the con

Trump tried to reverse votes in Wisconsin
Insisted state reps recount so he could win
He took their measure
Put on the pressure
But he lost despite this political shenanigan

Nevada and Arizona had more ballots to sort
Trump said my totals best not come up short
'Cuz here's the deal
I intend to appeal
If I don't win we're taking you to court

Mike Pence is an Indiana Hoosier
VP and an ass-kissing schmoozer
He sold his soul
To protect Trump's hole
Even God thinks he's a loser

And here's to the Dunce of Dense
Donald Trump's VP Mike Pence
Insipidly white
Not all that bright
He makes pudding look intense

Mike Pence is an Indiana Hoosier
VP and Donald's lackey and excuser
A fly in his hair
Another down there
He's the perfect ass-kissing schmoozer

Jim Jordan's a Republican pit bull
We know he'll never run out of fuel
No brown line on his brow
Neither before or now
No question of what he's so full

On 1/6 Trump and cronies caused a riot
After it happened they all tried to deny it
Republicans defend
The base pretend
It never happened but we don't buy it

Governors of Florida, S. Dakota and Texas
Don't seem to care if covid infects us
Such political liars
These covid deniers
Their policies continue to vex us

Seems there is really no end in sight
Of Republicans and Trump's blight
Can't really be sure
How long to endure
Before citizens and Congress see the light

While the January 6 committee investigates
The Department of Justice procrastinates
So slow to move
So long to prove
Republicans postulate, and Trump fabricates

TV media reports more Trump crimes
Also printed in the Post and the Times
Yet no charges laid
No price has been paid
While Trump picks those whom he primes

Another revelation released in the news
Trump's guilty of federal document abuse
Ripped them in pieces
Or flushed them like feces
Treating his presidential history as refuse

Trump's not the only thing at Mar-a-Lago
Fifteen boxes of document stored as cargo
But the DOJ
Says no way
They must reman here and not so far go

It is important for citizens to take note
Republicans pass state laws and they gloat
You'll get a screwing
With what they're doing
As they do everything to steal your vote

Trump and his kids now to be deposed
And all the dirty linen will be exposed
T'will not be brief
But will nail the thief
When the cell door slams they'll be enclosed

The Georgia call's been heard with the plea
Just find 1180 more votes and you'll see
I'll remain in power
Please do it now'er
You'll soon have to deal with me

Trump and his minions spout the BIG LIE
No surprises from the Orange Menace guy
But now the facts
Are revealing his acts
And when deposed if he lies he will fry

Don Jr. and Ivanka's deposition aren't set
Appeals and stalling will delay and yet
When all is done
There'll be three not one
Ensnared in daddy's criminal net

Ted Cruz believes he has balls of brass
He's personally and politically so crass
But we would saver
If he did all a favor
Bent over and put his head up his ass

The face of Mitch McConnell's sports
A dull, expressionless statement of sorts
If he should die
No wonder why
He already resembles a corpse

Lindsay Graham has a wayward mouth
His political switches are quite scouth
It should be ordered
He be drawn n' quartered
Distributed to north, east, west and south

DJ Trump really believed he was clever
But the New York DA's found a lever
She's got the facts
To lower the axe
And charge him for his criminal endeavor

Trump says his friend Vlad Putin's a genius
He's attacking Ukraine at his convenience
No good can come
Certainly not from
These two flawed egomaniacal deviants

Tucker Carlson's big mouth on Fox News
Spouts lies conspiracies and fake views
Whips up the masses
The poor dumb asses
His conspiracy theories are not an excuse

And it continues on and on
All the bullshit with the Don
The blonde guy
And his big lie
Are still just a big con

Roe v. Wade by SCOTUS has been struck
Best be careful if you continue to fuck
A period missed
And you'll be pissed
No place to go for a legal fetus pluck

What's with those nuts Clarence and Ginny
She likes how Long Dong Silver can whinny
She's so far right
He's a SCOTUS blight
And we all want to know the real skinny

SCOTUS has completed their contortion
Their intent is quite clear no distortion
Women are controlled
By the government's hold
As they limit their access to abortion

The wagons are circling for DJ Trump
Yet he continues to rant from his stump
Still getting by
Telling the great lie
Wrap it up and jam it far up his rump

So many Trump allies sought a pardon
Their guilt as obvious as a hard on
All sing the same song
We all did no wrong
Such bullshit could fertilize my garden

Down in Georgia the grand jury holds sway
It's subpoenaed both Rudy and Lindsay
Get them under oath
Then nail them both
And with Trump finally put them all away

US right whites are concerned about color
But with only them it would be duller
So red, black and brown
And yellow must go down
They all want to be the herd cull'er

When your GOP heads are stuck up your ass
You can only inhale n' breathe your own gas
So come up for air
There's a world out there
And we don't need any more of your crass

With a hey-nonney-nay and a tutt-frutti
They're going after the dishonored Rudy
Yes, it's about time
That this fallen slime
Should face the music and at last do his duty

The Donald's getting closer to prison
But he postures with disdain and derision
But nowhere to hide
Not his to decide
Charged and convicted not his decision

Trump seems to have merged with QUanon
But that's not a very smart move, Don
Too blind to see
It's a conspiracy
Flush them one and all down the john

The Feds searched his Mar-a-Lago resort
Found several hundred pages to sort
Claimed declassified
As usual he lied
And DOJ and DJT will be locked in court

Anything Trump touches he thinks is his
And that's that so no reason to quiz
DOJ says no
That ain't so
Return to the gov and you're getting the biz

So many Trump allies have taken the fifth
Their lies have them on the edge of the cliff
But they remain at large
Haven't been charged
Hey, Trump's still free so what's the diff

30 of Trump's close allies are on the block
Subpoenas could mean a loud door knock
You've been served
Long deserved
For sucking on Trump's political cock

For those still attached to Trump's teat
Elon Musk has restored his right to tweet
Gather those digits
All of you idjits
And tweet about this winning defeat

Republicans sit on their hands and are silent
No balls to resist Trump's stupid intent
Continue to cower
Seek only power
But citizens wonder where their souls went

Republicans still remain in Trump's shadow
How many more big elections must he blow
Not a boozer
Just a big loser
Now everyone in the USA should know

No Republicans reside in Trump's tower
But many still kiss his ass and cower
Without plan or platform
There remains but one norm
They want complete and absolute power

Trump promised a big major announcement
Media speculated on a new pronouncement
When it came
What a shame
The cards are a personal embarrASSment

Trump's own trading cards are now for sale
Even his friends and cronies went pale
They're mighty fine
Only ninety-nine
Was there ever such a self-adoring male

It's now clear that Trump has the hotsies
For right wing conspiracists and the Nazis
When they come to dine
It's really quite fine
There's a complete room full of nasties

White supremacists and Nazis were there
But Trump said I didn't know, it's not fair
I'm a true winner
They just came for dinner
And without denial his true self's laid bare

Trump stupidly took 1000's of documents
From the WH to his Mar-a-Lago residence
He took the line,
They're really mine
A record of my own presidential eminence

DJT's ego's so big he just doesn't accept it
That he stole presidential stuff n' shlepped it
I took it to Florida
'Cudda had moruvit
Because I want it, it's all mine and I kept it

When Trump's tried, convicted and in jail
No more wins but the beginning of fail
He'll hue and cry
I don't understand why
So I told lots of lies and had some free tail

Trump's business is guilty and convicted
We hope that it'll be fined and restricted
No more big deals
For these crooked wheels
All future business denied or restricted

Trump says who cares I just get stronger
But this creep and financial whore-monger
This king of dumb
May lose his freedom
And remain in federal custody much longer

And what of his Republican henchmen
What's the verdict for each of them then
Get'em together
And let'em never
Run or ever hold political office again

I wanted to buy Trump cards for myself
My kids could store them on a closet shelf
In fifty years
Their kid's peers
Would pay big and they'd get some wealth

For his cards Trump got 4.5 million bucks
Doesn't seem to matter how many he fucks
Over they bend
Take it in the end
So many stupid, ass kissing dumb clucks

Seems that DJT's empire will soon be gone
Left bereft and with a sentence quite long
No one will care
No one will be there
To listen to his lies and sad demented song

History won't be kind to Donald J. Trump
Books will sneer at the plump dumb chump
There could be many
But doubt there'll be any
To care if he's buried in an unmarked dump

What will Donald J. Trump's legacy be
History requires that we must wait and see
But now and today
So many would say
The worst anything of the land of the free

The wagons are circling and closing in
DJT has become a was and a has been
The fat-assed fool
Sits on his gold stool
Shits and thinks how to escape with his skin

The Jan 6 Committee has released its report
The DOJ must decide to charge or abort
DJT just gives his regards
Issues his pathetic cards
Drops his drawers and moons his retort

Trumpty-Dumpty had a great spasm
Fell off the wall into a deep chasm
No idea where
And really don't care
If he survived or the devil now has 'im

The NY courts got evidence and pounced
Donald's company is guilty on 17 counts
He doesn't care
Probably won't share
In whatever penalty's at last announced

I'm waiting for Garland and the DOJ
To charge DJ Trump and put him away
No access to bail
Put him in jail
To remain there until his death day

If Trump's convicted to spend time in a cell
He most certainly will not take it too well
Unable to wander
Much time to ponder
Just how far his pompous hair and ass fell

What happens to the Secret Service detail
Must they also protect Donald in jail
Forget it they said
I'll retire instead
Screw 'im, we're all going to bail

The wagons are circling the Feds closing in
On Trump and hopefully some of his kin
Don't get it wrong
It's taken so long
Hey Garland, where in hell have you been

Cruz-Haley-McCarthy-Green and Gaetz
House names who should be mutual inmates
Trump's loyal minions
No individual opinions
Are no better than what DJ Trump defecates

Trump continues his loud-mouthed denial
Of his wrong-doing and during his trial
Smirked with derision
Until the decision
No time in Mar-a-Lago for a long while

Trump said hey wait you can't do this to me
I'm the true president and a TV celebrity
No one fucks Don
I'm made of Teflon
No one has been able to convict or touch me

The House is a Republican embarrassment
The renegade ten made clear their intent
No votes today
McCarthy no way
No Speaker for you without our consent

They are now embarking on vote number 8
RNC losers still control McCarthy's fate
Just take note
How we vote
So a fraud and liar becomes a head of state

After 12 attempts McCarthy finally made it
For the right-wing deals he took a big a hit
But he doesn't care
Said I'm finally there
As Speaker he's tarnished and a real dipshit

And now they have something on Biden
Documents found in the house he resides in
It raises alarms
Republicans up in arms
To investigate the documents Biden's hidin'

Mostly likely Joe Biden never knew
And had little or nothing to do
Of his own had enough
No hand packing the stuff
When his tenure as VP was through

From the right loud howls are heard
Biden immediately called FBI and assured
T'was accidental error
An incidental bearer
That intentional possession was absurd

Trump's on the verge of being indicted
Hush money for Stormy and campaign cited
Republicans are critical
Complain it's political
But I couldn't possibly be more delighted

Trump says he will be arrested next Tuesday
This might be his day to sing the blues day
Years overdue
So screw you
Convict, jail and at last it is his fools-day

Republicans cry out and claim its foul play
The Democrats just want their political say
They'd be delighted
If Trump's indicted
Convicted and jailed will be a great day

The Orange Menace is finally indicted
One thing might make us more delighted
Guilty by his peers
Sentenced a few years
T'would make us even more excited

So what about Jan/6 and Georgia
DJT we never could really afford ya
You've had your day
When courts have their say
The government will room and board ya

Bragg and the grand jury have the last word
More lies from Trump are really absurd
He's mentally sick
Can't face the music
Just place him with the imprisoned herd

The GOP has started a big new go fund me
To raise millions to help defend DJT
The sonovabitch
Is already rich
So spend his millions for the legal fee

Trump will open his mouth and self-convict
He'll continue to protest loudly and depict
It's a Democrat stunt
A total witch hunt
He'll never admit he's finally been licked

The Republican colors are fully showing
Despite the truth which they're all knowing
Trump's a poor choice
Just a loud voice
But it's certainly his dick they're all blowing

The decision to indict Trump fills the news
There are diametrically opposing views
The GOP raises money
The Dems say honey
The sonofabitch is finally getting his dues

The court requires Mike Pence to appear
Must testify before the grand jury we hear
This wimpy muppet
DJT's puppet
Could make Trump's criminality quite clear

Pence must testify before the grand jury
But will he obfuscate to further curry
Trump's good will
Or had his fill
To respond with truth is DJT's big worry

When Trump unzipped and said, hey Stormy
Just looking at you makes me quite horny
I'm so aroused 'n
For $130,000
Would you please spread your legs for me

With women Trump was quite pushy
Said he could grab them by the pussy
But they replied
Let us be your guide
In shoving it up your own tushie

If you indict me there will certainly be
Lots of death and destruction you'll see
But if in a cell
Or sent to hell
Either way of DJ Trump we'll be free

No way to predict what will happen
Trump was certainly caught nappin'
He's gittin' his
Golly gee whiz
That's fear not shit that he's crappin'

Trump seems to think he's above it
I'm the real President and I love it
So try me
Deny me
But you can take it all and shove it

Trump thinks whatever we do he'll survive
Despite our frustration and anger he'll thrive
But if he's nailed
And finally jailed
We won't care whether he's dead or alive

It's time to be rid of DJ Trump and his shit
Try and convict him and then make him sit
In a 3'x3' cell
Right next to hell
The correct size for his ego to fit

Trump's incarceration won't be good
He'll claim he was just misunderstood
He'll rot in a cell
And scream like hell
When his roommate slips him the wood

Donald Trump is having a really hard time
That he's finally been indicted is sublime
And he should worry
That the judge and jury
Will make him accountable for his crime

Trump is a loud-mouthed bully and pushy
In future there's no MacDonald's or sushi
Confined to a cell
In his personal hell
He might become his bunkmate's pussy

Despite all the crimes Trump's denyin'
His claims of innocence we're not buyin'
The Orange Menace
Really offends us
He's definitely not a lamb but a lyin'…..
SONUVABITCH

Trump's off to New York and must answer
Please try convict and remove this man, sir
Where his ugly orange face
And the wardrobe of the place
Will be a color-coded match in the can, sir

DJ Trump thinks that he is untouchable
That everyone, like him, is corruptible
He's screwed so many
If there's justice any
Off to Rykers where he'll be fuckable

Trump is fingerprinted but no mug shot
Just as well with the orange mug he's got
Then into court
His time there short
His first chance to plead guilty or not

In court Donald has no personal choice
He has no reason to be proud and rejoice
First Potus indicted
So many delighted
He'll likely self-convict with his voice

At last Trump's moment has come
It's taken too long for me and some
Tried at last
For sins past
We can hopefully be rid of this bum

In New York Trump surrendered for arrest
Marjorie Taylor Green went there to protest
Her presence short
He stood in court
As at least some of his crimes are addressed

Trump's indictment led him to fluster Attacks
on the DA and judge he did muster
Not guilty he said
That's how he pled
Then later shouted more lies and bluster

His supporters are so deaf, blind and gaga
Continue to worship and support his saga
The poor sod
Thinks he's God
And all his disciples are members of MAGA

Trump claims that every investigation
Is just a Democratic political frustration
I am the Messiah
I'm the only guy ya
Want as the head of your nation

Oh Donald, Oh Donald, wherefore art thou
Is that sweat on your frightened orange brow
The NY DA
Has found the way
To convict you with solid facts now

The NY judge asked both sides to be quiet
But Trump immediately spoke up to defy it
He defamed the DA
The judge the same day
If gagged by the judge he'll decry it

In NY the judge asked both sides for silence
But Trump's Florida words were in defiance
Cannot maintain
Control of his brain
Without a gag there'll be no compliance

Trump's mouth has no route to his brain
It's not his fault he can't seem to restrain
There is no doubt of it
What comes out of it
Causes not the slightest brain drain

Lindsey Graham was on TV with his pleas
Please give Trump money to pay legal fees
Ignore him
Deplore him
He's worth less than a fart on the breeze

For those keeping Trump daily in the media
Stop, inform him we've no more needuvya
Just tell him NO
Get your own show
How we'd all love to be totally relieveduvya

If Lindsey has another switch in his position
We'll know he's made a Trumpian decision
I've sold my soul
To the Orange asshole
Like MAGA, I'm in total submission

Trump asked his army to gather in rejection It
can only be fraud if I lost this election
Gather the troupes
Come in large groups
Let's take over the capitol by insurrection

Did you see what happened in Tennessee
Jim Crow's alive and black reps aren't free
To express views held
They were expelled
The white lady rep only one left of the three

A racist Jim Crow message from Tennessee
Keep your black mouth shut or you'll see
If your not compliant
Don't remain silent
We'll take you out to visit the state tree

If Trump's MAGA, white rights and others
Were allowed to have all their d'rothers
All the colored races
'D remain in their places
Or they'd all sleep underneath sod covers

Donald Trump's tongue has openly wagged
On 5th Avenue I could shoot you he bragged
I would go on
Being the Don
As you went to the morgue and were tagged

If Donald continues to let his tongue wag
Blames everyone else and continues to brag
If the judge budges
Trump begrudges
I'm famous, so screw you and your gag

If Trump's rhetoric gets bad and red-flagged
The judge says shut up you've been gagged
Fed up to the brim
Best not ignore him
Or be arrested, snagged, dragged, n' bagged

If you want to silence this orange faced twit
Sew his lips together so he can't even spit
While you've got 'im
Sew up his bottom
Then he'll most definitely be full of shit

Open up Trump's head to see what it yields
It won't be surprising to see what it shields
Beneath the hair
There's enough there
To fertilize ALL of America's fields

Trump continues to speak out and fumes
Believes he is Teflon and always assumes
No matter what
Kiss my butt
I raise the ratings in all the newsrooms

All of Graham, McCarthy, and Jordan rants
Stir legal waters to improve Trump's chance
But all they expose
As everyone knows
Is their brains are concealed by their pants

It's taken too long for our flawed democracy
To destroy Trump and all his hypocrisy
Thinks he's the right
Because he is white
To be king of an American autocracy

If Trump runs again we must foil it
Get many more voters to spoil it
We must beat him
Badly defeat him
And then flush him down his golden toilet

Trump is convinced that he's far too rich
That none of his cohorts would ever snitch
Break all their ties
Tell truth to his lies
And help convict the orange son of a bitch

With regard to the U football nuclear
To Mr. Trump it should never be near
He's too cavalier
And quite insincere
And it increases my angst and my fear

GOP judges considering medical provisions
Must follow the logic of their own decisions
If they are sick
They get to pick
Where they start cutting their own incisions

Concerning Trump the GOP is not astute
It doesn't require a genius to compute
Every adult
In this GOP cult
Continues to function as his prostitute

Trump claims that NY officials were crying
But new pictures as usual show he was lying
The way he looked
After he was booked
Was wonderful and so gratifying

Trump lives in a self-centered universe
Hard to imagine how he could get worse
Best hold your breath
Wait for his death
He's been the US's worst home-grown curse

When deposed Trump took the 5th 450 times
Screw the grand jury and its paradigms
I haven't done
A single one
It's a witch hunt, I've committed no crimes

Trump says his problems are just a smear
The democrats simply want me to disappear
For my defense
Send dollars and cents
To the go fund me page listed here

Trump said it amazes but no longer stuns me
That despite my wealth these fools fund me
They send it
So I spend it
Saving me millions of my own money

All these attacks are a democratic stunt
Smearing my integrity is a personal affront
There's nothing to repent
I'm completely innocent
And the law is now part of the witch hunt

Trump says I'm an equal opportunity thief
I steal from everybody so what's your beef
If you're bereft
Have nothing left
You can always just go on relief

Where have you been living the last while
Those with great power use it then smile
This is now
We know how
And honor and integrity are just out of style

Trump has the MAGA folk under his spell
They want me President for life I can tell
W-f-a-y
There's no "f" in way
That's what I said so please go to hell

In NY DJT's business is on trial for fraud His
bookkeeping practices are quite flawed
If justice holds sway
And then takes away
250 million then we'll all cheer and applaud

Donald Trump has attended good schools
But like other illiterate and ignorant fools
It's no embarrassment
Damned right I'm arrogant
I'm also brilliant and above all the rules

The golden rule is a rule for all men
They do unto you as you do unto them
Time for the Trumps
To take their lumps
So lets screw them over and over again

No longer President Trump's just a mister
It's time he should lose, no longer a victor
It won't be funny
Take all his money
Then convict and jail this disgusting grifter

Jim Jordan is nothing but a Trump pit bull
His actions and words are contemptible
He flusters and sneers
Blusters and fears
But privately he knows he's just shit full

Trump's own words indicate he's a retard
For the truth he demonstrates no regard
So if he testifies
He will tell lies
And end up hoisted on his own petard

Everyone knows Trump's tongue is his foe
Whatever comes out of it is usually faux
Searched in vain
Didn't find his brain
The space filled only by a giant ego

As a stable genius DJ Trump was hired
Shoveling horseshit the only thing required
But he was inept
And wasn't kept
Told you're not worth shit so you're fired

More Republicans throw hats in the ring
Seeking to dethrone the orange-blonde king
When said and done
There's not a one
Offering something new or worth anything

Trump continues to remain the orange peril
A braggart, a bully, loud-mouthed and oral
Cease and desist
We're really pissed
That you're so totally, completely amoral

For others Trump has absolutely no regard
He should be hoisted with his own petard
And if you please
Brought to his knees
All business, politics n' government barred

No avenues left so Pence has at last spoken
The judge has ruled and his silence is broken
Might be the fix
For January 6
Where the special counsel's been pokin'

After so long and so slowly are we at last
Hearing unassailable evidence is amassed
There'll be a charge
P'raps no longer at large
Trump will face all the crimes of his past

The Justice Department seems in no hurry
To indict Trump and bring him before a jury
We'd like to know
Why they're so slow
They only add to our outrage and fury

Proud Boys may regret statements out loud
As their 1/6 actions put them under a cloud
They've been tried
Let the jury guide
Their joining of the US penal crowd

Trump and the far right want to disavow
Laws which have provisions that do allow
Women's redress
To abortion access
And no say over their bodies, RIGHT NOW

Americans are suffering from severe myopia
They're no longer living in a USA utopia
Actions and discourse
Without any remorse
Have clearly resulted in national dystopia

For the approaching US Presidential election
The GOP has a growing group for selection
Please take note
Be sure to vote
Make sure they all receive a total rejection

The Presidential election for the year 2024
Could decide democracy's future and more
Finally capture
Possibly fracture
The home of the brave and free to its core

Trump, Haley, Atkinson, and Ramaswamy
Pence, DeSantis, Scott part of the tsunami
Messaging rings
There are more in the wings
For who will survive, you consult a swami

So many are concerned over Joe Biden's age
The politicians and pundits continue to rage
Lift your voice
Make a choice
Trump mustn't return to the national stage

We're living a dangerous time in US history
Too many dreadful things on the list for me
No end in sight
From the far right
A democratic hysterectomy isn't a mystery

If the GOP right-wingers get their d'rothers
They'll change laws to suit all their brothers
Forget all the rest
We know what's best
So shut up while we screw all the others

It seems clear what the Republicans intend
They want to bring democracy to an end
Don't doubt it
They even flout it
And they sure as hell aren't your friend

The American public is under serious duress
And it's not difficult to ponder why or guess
Trump and his minions
And their right opinions
Are largely responsible for creating the mess

Can Trump should he win govern from jail
What special arrangements would this entail
Can a convict
Sign an edict
Can the warden censure a President's mail

If the DA in Georgia finally indicts in July
Will we see from all the legal violations why
DJ Trump's guilt
Was solidly built
On the foundation of his own truly Big Lie

On 1/6 Pence refused to deny or waver
Give in to Trump's demand for a favor
Ignored the slight
Did what's right
About the only VEEP action he can savor

What solution is there for the US violence
It's past time for gun laws no more silence
It could be you
Next in the cue
Either through accident, choice or chance

Give us a break and put orange man down
Tar n' feather'im n' run'im out of town
We've had enough
What he's so full of
Should make his color completely brown

Trump's responsible for MAGA's seduction
Who back his words and acts of corruption
Of like kind
Or just blind
To his achieving democracy's destruction

Politicians might finally go aftert the guns
Squash the NRA n' cease taking their funds
When blood's spilled
The next ones killed
Include their moms, dads, daughters or sons

We must find a way to be rid of DJT
If not out in the open at least on the QT
No matter how or who
It should be PDQ
Maybe today, yesterday, definitely ASAP

When politicians' families end up deceased
The gun and NRA support might be ceased
At last feel remorse
Change their course
Their support for gun removals increased

A bird in hand is better than one over head
A gun in hand means a victim could be dead
Take them away
It's not at all okay
No more sales and reclaim all others instead

When born he was named Donald John
He decided to match his namesake Don Juan
Lowered his britches
Diddled the bitches
I'm not just your ordinary millionaire john

DJT claims that E. Jean Carrol's not a cutie
She's not my type and she's not a beauty
I would require
A bit more fire
Before I'd be willing to go after her booty

When Donald's finally cornered and begs
Remember his head holds only last dregs
The last of his brains
The few he retains
Are located in the head between his legs

Know what that silly blonde flop shields
Enough fertilizer to enrich all of the fields
So no excuse
Let's put it to use
It might even improve some crop yields

I guess we'd all better just tighten our belts
Shhh until hell freezes or all the ice melts
Believe as they do
Or they'll come for you
It's their way, the highway or else

How have we arrived at this dangerous place
And it's getting worse at a snowballing pace
The right white
May be the plight
Which exterminates the entire human race

A wolf in sheep's clothing has them gaga
Wrapped in the lies of his political life saga
While he deceives
The flock believes
Welcome to the Trump cult named MAGA

Trump is a self-made arrogant ignoramus
Now for all the wrong reasons he's famous
But his cupidity
And his stupidity
Has nationally n' internationally shamed us

Donald J. Trump is a walking living disaster
Of guile, lies and deceit he is the master
If the GOP
And Mr. DJT
Are elected America's demise will be faster

We all watched Trump descend the stair
Flaunting the flop and arrogance with flair
But if you bare
What little's there
It's just bullshit, bad manners and hot air

Trump truly believes that he's royalty
While you are lower than his toiletry
When his sins are exposed
He turns up his nose
Still demands complete and total loyalty

It's clear Trump is unburdened by his guilt
From his youth it's just the way he was built
But if he's tested
Finally arrested
Tried, convicted and incarcerated he'll wilt

This craven narcissist fills 1000s of pages
Hours of radio n' TV on the world's stages
Time to retire
Even better fire
This Trumpian disaster is one for the ages

Trump will not appear at the Carrol trial
He's gone off to Scotland for a while
A new course will be
For his balls on a tee
As for all the charges at home he's in denial

May the Scots all boycott Trump's club
Give it a cold shoulder and a complete snub
It's better I think
To have a drink
Maybe some darts and a few pints at the pub

When they took x-rays of Trump's head
They were immediately developed and read
What was discovered
What x-rays uncovered
Only three brain cells alive, the rest dead

Trump wants to think he's in total command
He'll get everything he wants and planned
If he were to fail
And end up in jail
He and supporters will equally be damned

Has the American democracy run its course
The right-wing is rushing to rabidly endorse
Political insurrection
An earlier direction
Of puritanical laws and conditions by force

Some members of SCOTUS have lost face
Recent revelations have struck at their base
They tasted the fruit
Accepted the loot
Before citizens, God and country a disgrace

DJT, GOP n' SCOTUS keep their defiance
Equally corrupt in their acts and compliance
Drive them from office
No need to be cautious
They screwed us all. it's not rocket science

The US says that it is a nation of laws
A statement often met with some guffaws
But not from the rich
Or powerful which
Seem exempt from guilt and all just because

There're some things we haven't missed
That make us angry and politically pissed
Too many reps
Took wrong steps
And support only the asses they've kissed

The ultra right's passing laws of no worth
To control books, LGBTQ, voting and birth
When they're done
Seem to have won
One more step right, they'll fall off the earth

If Trump regains power he said he intends
To burn everyone not counted as friends
I will deploy
Group and destroy
Everyone on the list and reap my revenge

Some reports say Trump's scared to death
That makes us so sad and totally bereft
Still he just could
Escape if he would
Just indefinitely hold his last breath

As the indictments increasingly mount
Several suits and cases by my count
Trump's gonna fall
Can't escape all
Far too many for his lawyer's to surmount

Should Trump become President once more
You should be terrified deep to the core
He's said what he plans
Take all in his hands
So vote like you know what you're in for

Elected, Trump's stated what will happen
Attention voters, don't be caught nappin'
He wants to be king
Able to do anything
So be sure to vote and send him packin'

Trump's Congressional cult is up to its neck
So few honest GOPs so let's clear the deck
Vote all of them out
'Cuz democracy's about
Keeping all the power seekers in check

As America struggles to regain its hold
Bring power mongers back into the fold
Absolutely emperical
They need a miracle
For something dramatic, drastic and bold

At Trump's rallies he's ranter and whiner
Should be ignored and sent to his recliner
And for your ear
Hear it here
His complete disappearance would be finer

Mr. Trump, if you always do things right
Why so nervous so clearly up tight
Loosen your shorts
Here come the courts
In complete orange you'll be a great sight

Trump's Presidency is one for the books
When convicted we'll see what it brooks
There'll be no mystery
Your place in history
Will be among America's greatest crooks

Mr. Trump you are a self-made criminal
You're a disastrous political original
No longer at large
When the courts charge
The maximum sentence not the minimal

Quit asking God to eliminate this prick
In 2024 make your vote politic
Vote for whomever
But for Trump never
Just take care for which box that you tick

DJT's cult has so much dirty laund-a-ry
What should their essential squander be
They should dump
Mr. DJ Trump
Solving the mess of their own quan-da-ry

Trump showed others top secret documents
His voice on the tape is clear evidence
For an ignorant fool
Who thinks it's cool
To admit on tape a national security offence

Should Trump's current run be successful
America's future will be quite unrestful
The orange autocrat
And 77 year old brat
Will drown the US in his own cesspool

So many fools are born every day
Please don't let this one have his way
Trump must be stopped
Then photoshopped
And incarcerated for a long prison stay

Wish Trump had happened in a different life
Perhaps someone should approach his wife
Do us a favor
One we can savor
Go to the kitchen and find a sharp knife

The blonde mop atop the orange melon
Will be convicted as a criminal felon
Trump the ex Pres
Will have a new res
And be dragged off rebellin' and yellin'

The American political scene is a disaster
The far right fools ensure it collapses faster
Please intercede
Don't let them succeed
Put Trump and Republicans out to pasture

So much is said and written of this dunce
Wish DJT was gone from our presence
No one would grieve
If he'd just leave
Or accidentally speak the truth just once

Trump said I am the only one who can fix it
I'll cancel democracy and then deep six it
I'll be the boss
That's your loss
Agree or you know where you can stick it

The Republicans have pulled every lever
But the Clintons must be much more clever
Nothing would stick
Couldn't convict
Hate them but kiss Trump's ass forever

Florida will teach kids slavery's benefits
Each class will learn only the "good" bits
Forget the rest
Not on the test
History rewritten by white redneck twits

If Trump's permitted to have his way
When re-elected he'll permanently stay
The aged brat
And autocrat
Will continue to destroy the US of A

Trump ignores everyone's rights with ease
I can do anything, whatever I please
Kick his behind
Get him confined
And permanently brought to his knees

History will record Donald Trump's infamy
His crimes will be a long, lengthy litany
The US was cursed
Led by the worst
If there's a devil he's clearly the epitomy

Once and for all let it be over and done
The DOJ convicts and jails the orange one
For his crime
Serve his time
And never be allowed to again see the sun

America has experienced enough of error
Don't re-elect the Republican flag bearer
Take good note
Mark your vote
Or there'll be a disastrous reign of terror

When the far-right Republicans convene
Their actions and comments are obscene
Lies and conspiracy
Political tyranny
Destroy democracy and freedom in between

My thoughts of Donald Trump are unclean
In fact they're downright nasty and obscene
He's the master
A one man disaster
Love'im or hate'im there's no in between

The Republican party has gone to sleep
Paid no attention to the company they keep
Been bulldozed
Politically hozed
And become the flock of Trump's sheep

We can hope that the Trump era will pass
Be done with this arrogant bully of crass
T'would be a boon
If it was soon
Choke on a burger then bury his fat ass

Trump believes he's a mover and shaker
But he's no giver he's only a taker
If he should die
Let him lie
He won't be going to meet his maker

Donald J Trump is so full of shit
An ignorant pompous bully and twit
And when he dies
Wherever he lies
I will be pleased and not care a whit

Trump's like the deadly water moccasin
Wish the media would put a pox on him
Removed from the air
Silent everywhere
The rest of us could use the oxygen

Trump's name is on the air every hour
Impossible to escape this verbal shower
Turn off his mic
Is what I'd like
And dimmish a big source of his power

Trump loves his burgers, fries and coke
Which for him might result in a stroke
And after you eat
Get off your feet
Just lie down, roll over and croak

In bridge trump cards are in control
DJ Trump wants to fill the same role
He'll not do well
As resident in hell
'Cuz the devil will still own his soul

Trump's really gotten inside of my head
Anyone else would have been better instead
Feels like I'm cursed
But it could be reversed
If he were discovered dead in his bed

When he dies Trump should not lie in state
A decision that should require no debate
In his case
It's not the place
For a disgusting liar 'n promoter of hate

If Trump's parents had not procreated
Donald's future wouldn't be debated
There'd be no fear
He was never here
Nothing at all to be related

To be hung by the neck until dead
A sentence that criminals used to dread
But Trump needs more time
To ponder his crime
So he should be hung by his balls instead

When Trump's gone, dead or replaced
How long before the bad memory's erased
Will the party of Lincoln
Rediscover their thinkin'
Expunge the far-right and MAGA disgraced

Fulton County's indicted Trump in Georgia
When convicted I'm sure they'll accord ya
Treat 'ya like shit
You won't like it
That Georgia gets to room and board ya

What's going on with President Biden
Is he campaigning or politically hide'n
Needs a firm plan
To attack the orange man
And secure 4 years in the WH he abides in

Trump's Georgia criminal mug shot
Attempts to threaten but it ain't so hot
Attempts to conceal
The fear he can feel
In face of all the charges he's now got

Trump is finally going down for the count
Years in prison and sued a big dollar amount
Let him disappear
No longer here
His incarceration long and pronounced

Is Pence really that politically dense
After so many years riding the fence
Must suffer discomfort
Don't your balls hurt
Stand up and use common sense

There's a reason for Trump being so thick
For being a preposterous, pompous prick
His brains are located
Where he masterbated
Right there in the smaller head of his dick

Here's to D.J. Trump the King of Slime
Master of all forms of white-collar crime
He has invented
More than you've prevented
And truly believes he'll never do time

Will the DOJ ever arrest DJT's tail
Then permit him to also post bail
Let's hope not
That it's got
More balls and puts the bastard in jail

Trump continues to hold rally after rally
Far too many for anyone to tally
But all he can muster
Is more bullshit and bluster
Sliding down the throats of MAGA alley

Melania told Donald if you run again dear
Do not expect Baron or myself to appear
Don't' bother to ask
We've no part in the task
Even if you kiss my beautiful round rear

We can only shake our heads and wonder
How Donald has ripped US politics asunder
This lothario cupid
Who is so stupid
Continues to make blunder after blunder

The Majority Leader's a son of a bitch
Was answering a question during which
His brain blanked
Suddenly tanked
We're wondering where you went, Mitch

Mitch says there's nothing wrong with me
Just occasionally like to set my brain free
Take a mind trip
Get a fresh grip
To escape some of this political debris

As for Donald J. Trump there is no solution
He's definitely real and not a delusion
Wish it weren't so
That he'd just go
This disgusting piece of human pollution

Donald calls him Ron De Sanctimonious
Has no personality and quite acrimonious
Changing the rules
Taking over schools
Claims a large following, that's erroneous

In history these figures seem to appear
To generate masses with hatred and fear
Regardless their time
The extent of their crime
We could only wish they weren't here

While Trump continues his endless tirade
He's planning his 2nd presidential parade
We need to wake up
And need to shake up
The citizenry as his intent's not a charade

While its much worse than a donkey braying
Best listen closely to what Trump is saying
When next selected
If he's duly elected
It's you and democracy he'll be betraying

The end of US democracy could be in sight
Citizens of conscience must stand and fight
Trump must go
Please vote no
Elect a more qualified person, please unite

A NY judge has stirred up Trump's ire
Closing down DJTs New York empire
The start of a deluge
With no visible refuge
For this bogus ex-Pres and highflyer

Donald Trump's world is beginning to fail
So many state and federal courts on his tail
You've been a disaster
You stupid bastard
So off to jail with no chance for bail

With 91 criminal charges in four courts
Small wonder Donald is a bit out of sorts
A guilty finding
Will be binding
And his confinement in prison enforced

Trump had the nuclear pouch on his knee
A burger, fries, coke and watching TV
Here's the deal
I'm the big wheel
And you'd better take me seriously

DJT was bored watching TV on the couch
I really have questions and my own doubts
About the contents
And his intents
About what's inside of this nuclear pouch

Donald Trump claims to be a world genius
But really a liar and filled with sneakiness
Don't be misled
About his head
It's only there for his hairs' convenience

A marvel of engineering sits on his head
Does he spray it, comb it or feed it instead
What keeps that hair
Sitting up there
The secret is glue plus needles and thread

McCarthy's Speakership was a GOP waste
His the blame for the opposition he faced
Slaked his political ego
But first Speaker to go
And be voted out and thrown by the Gaetz

In New York Trump's on trial for fraud
No matter how much he hemmed and hawed
Out came the facts
Bogus values and tax
At last something we can happily applaud

Since Trump plans another run let's spoil it
At every twist and turn we should foil it
It would be fitting
If he's s(h)itting
To then flush him down his golden toilet

Mr. Trump this is the end of your time
For your businesses, politics and crime
Please disappear
Don't remain here
Slip back into the primordial slime.

Printed in the United States
by Baker & Taylor Publisher Services